FILM AND TV: THE WAY IN

A Guide to Careers

Robert Angell

BFI Publishing

First published in 1988 by the
British Film Institute
21 Stephen Street
London W1P 1PL

Copyright © Robert Angell 1988
Revised and reprinted 1989

Typeset by KC Graphics Ltd., Shrewsbury
Printed and bound in Great Britain by
St Edmundsbury Press,
Bury St Edmunds, Suffolk

British Library Cataloguing in Publication Data

Angell, Robert
    Film and TV: the way in: a guide to careers.
    1. Great Britain. Cinema industries & television film industries
    I. Title II. British Film Institute
    384′.8′0941

ISBN 0-85170-218-X

Contents

Contents

Foreword

SIR RICHARD ATTENBOROUGH
Chairman, British Film Institute

In spite of recurrent crises in film and television production, most of us who work in these industries would not have settled for any other career. But guidance for the many people I meet who would like to follow us along our chosen path has been scanty and not always helpful.

It is for this reason that I welcome the publication of *Film and TV: The Way In*. It is written from a completely practical standpoint by an experienced documentary film and video producer who himself has helped many people make a start in film and television. To those of us already involved, working in film or television remains a most invigorating and exciting life; to those who aspire to join us, I should like to wish every success.

Preface

As a Film and Video Producer for over twenty years, I have been on the receiving end of letters from hundreds of people: from school leavers and graduates, actors and stage designers, from writers and amateur movie-makers, all of whom want 'to get into films or television'.

Though happy to offer advice, I am frequently amazed at their ignorance of the basic structure of the film and television industries, not to mention how to set about getting a job there. It is to those seeking such information that this book is addressed, so that with it, anyone with the requisite amounts of persistence, ambition, talent, cheek and good luck may be able to gain a foothold in the industry on the way to becoming a future doyen of film and television.

Acknowledgements

I am extremely grateful to the following for their help and encouragement in the preparation of this book:

To Adrian Cooper for the draft of 'Anatomy of a Television
Production', to Colin Young and the National Film and Television
School, to Dick Ross, formerly at the Royal College of Art Department
of Film, and to all the other training establishments I have consulted.
To Anne Rawcliffe-King of the ACTT, Ian Wall of Film Education and
Bob Longman, formerly of the Howard Steele Foundation. To
Malcolm Davis, formerly Head of BBC Recruitment Services, and his
colleagues and to Robert Neal, formerly Head of Engineering and
Technical Operations Recruitment at the BBC. To Geoffrey Nowell-
Smith, Ed Buscombe and John Pym at the British Film Institute. And
finally, to all those who so willingly told me how they got started.

1

The Film and Television Industries

There is still, unfortunately, something of a gulf between the film and television industries, albeit one that is closing up all the time. On either side, the personnel form fairly tight-knit communities, operating in a series of small cell-like 'cottage industries' within the larger structure. There is certainly some cross-fertilisation taking place, both inside the cells and from one cell to another, but anyone wishing to enter the industry from the outside should be aware of how it is structured, what the various departments are and what are the jobs within these departments. With this basic knowledge, would-be applicants can then ascertain which sections appeal to them and for which they think they are most suitable. There is nothing wrong, of course, with wanting to be wholly involved in all the creative processes of making a film or television programme. Nowadays, however, the size and technical complexity of such operations mean that it is seldom possible, as once it was, for a single individual to come up with the original idea, write the script, load the camera, direct the action, shoot the scenes, process and edit the footage and then show the result to an audience, financing the whole operation from beginning to end and then making enough money at the end to show a little profit. Like it or not, film and television are now 'Industries', with all the corporate complexities and various levels of personnel which that involves.

The various broad divisions within the industries are: Feature Films, Documentary and Short Films, Television and Cinema Commercials, Animation, Television Production, Video Production and Workshops.

So to start with basics. There is film, photographic images and

1

sound preserved on a continuous strip of celluloid. And there is television, in which the images are produced electronically and recorded on magnetic tape. Films, of course, may be converted into television pictures and broadcast over the air; and increasingly the film industry is exploring the possibilities of replacing celluloid by video. But at the moment the technical differences between film and television do correspond roughly to differences between separate industries. At one end of the spectrum are full-length feature films made for showing in cinemas. All over the world, these are almost invariably made and shown in 35mm. film. At the other end are live television programmes broadcast in one country by ground-based transmitters or through satellite links across the world.

Between these two extremities lies the whole gamut of production, from modest or off-beat feature films for cinema release, made and shown on 16mm. film, through documentaries and films and videos for specialised audiences, to commercials for cinemas and television, made on film or video, to animated films and videos and, of course, the whole range of television production: drama, documentary, current affairs, education, children's programmes or sport. All of these may originate on 35 or 16mm. film or on video or be live television.

However broad the range, there is one thing common to all: the final aim is to produce moving pictures with sufficient visual and aural impact to affect the audience emotionally. But within the broad outlines of the film and television industries we may make some useful divisions.

1   Feature Films

These are made primarily for exhibition in cinemas, usually with actors and with a running time of at least ninety minutes. Productions are usually based at studios, such as Pinewood, Shepperton or Twickenham. Such studios these days have only a limited permanent staff, mainly concerned with the actual running of the studio: management, accounting, construction (although specific productions often have their own construction staff), projection, maintenance and catering. The bigger studios also employ resident recording engineers

2

and ancillary staff for the recording of music and sound effects, the post-synchronisation of dialogue, and dubbing.

A feature film company is often set up only for a single production, moving in to a studio only for the duration of the operation and hiring staff either from the studio or, as is more common, on a freelance basis for the production period. Opportunities for the newcomer are rare in such situations, though there may be exceptions in the case of large productions, where there is the possibility of short-term vacancies.

Similarly, periodic vacancies may occur in the most junior administrative jobs of a studio's permanent staff. Many of today's eminent film-makers started their careers as a studio messenger or third projectionist, and any school leaver determined to get into feature film production would be well advised to snap up any such job on offer. There is still plenty to be said for the time-honoured apprenticeship which results in an inside knowledge of the business and the people in it. Even those aspirants who are older and with academic qualifications should be prepared to follow a similar course, provided their ambitions allow them to endure menial work and low wages.

Feature film (or television) art departments may have vacancies for trainee draughtsmen or may even be prepared to take on designers of proven ability and talent. This is one of the few technical areas of the film and television industries where prior training or experience in allied fields (architecture, interior or stage design) may not only be of great benefit but may also prove to be useful as something to fall back on in times of sparse production.

2 Documentary and Short Films

Apart from those produced specifically for and by major television companies such as the BBC, most documentary and short films are made by small, self-contained companies. These can vary from a single talented and experienced producer/director working from a home base to the more elaborate set-ups with permanent staff and some technical facilities. Most of the latter are based in London, usually operating from Soho, which is still the traditional centre for every type of British film-making, distribution and marketing.

Documentary companies employ free-lancers for much of the time: these include writers, directors, camera crews, sound recordists, assistant directors, editors and assistant editors. Much of the work done by these companies (whether small, medium or large) is of a specialised nature, produced for sponsors such as government departments or industrial firms. Such films could be for sales purposes, for training, safety and recruiting, or for general information and public relations. A very few short films are made purely for entertainment, aimed at release as a supporting programme for cinema exhibition, but the hazards of distribution make this a very risky enterprise. Some documentary companies make films for television (see the section on Television below) but, again, the problems of getting adequate distribution worldwide, and hence adequate returns to cover the cost of production, limits expansion in this area. There is some hope, however, that new outlets, especially video-disc and cassette, cable, satellite and pay television, could lead to growth in the production side of this section of the industry. And now the firm commitment of the BBC and ITV companies to sub-contract a percentage of work to independent companies is further encouragement.

In recent years the documentary side of the industry has expanded dramatically, with higher standards in portable video cameras and video editing, and a new phrase has entered the vocabulary of sponsored production – corporate video. The main point about such production is that all shooting and editing is carried out on video, and the final use of the programme is normally restricted to videocassette, which is simple to use and cheap to duplicate. There may, however, be advantages in the original production being made on film and videocassette copies being made for release from this.

From time to time there may be opportunities of employment for newcomers as trainees in the cutting room or video editing suites, as messengers or as secretaries, which could in turn lead to a closer involvement in production.

3 Television and Cinema Commercials

As is the case with documentary production, the size of companies varies, but they are normally founded on the talent and reputation of those directors who are currently most in favour with the advertising agencies. Hence it has been known for people to find a way into production or directing via a job in the television department of an advertising agency. In commercials, most of the technical crew are engaged on a free-lance basis. There are some companies which provide only an editing service, and these, depending on the number of editors working for them, may have employment for the occasional assistant editor, trainee or messenger. Companies providing film edge-numbering and negative cutting services also may have vacancies for junior grades where there is a chance for newcomers to get used to handling film and to familiarise themselves with the editing and completion process of film-making.

As with documentaries the use of video both for shooting and editing has expanded enormously and the number of companies offering such shooting and editing facilities to producers has proliferated, with a corresponding increase in job opportunities for newcomers.

4 Animation

The process of production of an animated film overlaps many other areas of the industry, although the technique itself and consequently most of the jobs are unique. Animation may be used in title sequences for feature films or television programmes, in the design and layout of the titles themselves, in commercials, in diagrams and animated sequences as a part of documentaries, or, finally, as a complete film in its own right, perhaps only a few minutes long or perhaps a full-length feature such as *Watership Down.*

The style of the artwork and design reflects the style of the principal artist/animator, who therefore becomes the director. The more routine ancillary action and the backgrounds are dealt with by artists who may be recent art school graduates. The soundtracks of animated films are invariably very important and most animation production companies, therefore, have their own editing facilities.

The final stage in the making of an animated film is the photography of the artwork on a Rostrum camera. The work of the Rostrum cameraperson,* whilst not creative in the same way as other camerawork, demands an enormous amount of patience, precision and orderliness, as well as some idea of the complexity of the machinery which is being used. Some animation companies have their own Rostrum cameras and staff, whilst other companies offer a Rostrum camera service for animators who either do not have their own equipment or whose equipment is already fully occupied. For the newcomer coming from a film and animation course, a job as the camera assistant on a Rostrum camera could be a good starting point.

Computer graphics are a recent development in the field of animation and are largely geared to use on video, although systems exist whereby 1000-line video may be transferred to film with sufficient quality for projecting on to a large screen. Work in this field demands practical experience of computers and knowledge of graphic design. The possibilities for development in the field of abstract art are enormous and any art student wishing to obtain 'hands on' experience should try to make contact with someone operating in the field.

5 Television

The BBC and the Independent Television companies are the largest employers of all grades of production staff in Britain. Many of the jobs are permanent or at least on a contract for a series of programmes. Appointments of trainees and newcomers are highly regularised and usually handled through personnel departments. Although the BBC run their own excellent training schemes, the Independent Television companies have nothing comparable, for the simple reason that the companies are totally separate, each of them under different ownership, of varying size and operating in different ways and with different equipment. Consequently, there is no co-ordinated method of taking on newcomers. The ITVA (Independent Television Association) is

* 'Cameraperson' may be an ungainly term, but it is surely preferable to the unthinking use of 'cameraman' to describe a job which, though still mainly performed by men, can be and increasingly is carried out by women.

increasingly centralising its training, although much of this is for people already working for the independent companies rather than for newcomers. The whole business of training and trade unions will be dealt with later on.

The inception of Channel Four and the growth of international outlets such as satellite and cable have led to an increase in the number of independent production companies, often formed by people who have left the BBC or Independent Television companies or who have expanded from sponsored and corporate programmes into television production.

Television production techniques are divided roughly between film and video. Video is used mainly in areas of light entertainment, some drama and outside broadcasts; video therefore encompasses all the studio production jobs and, as far as direction and cameras are concerned, operations are entirely electronically based. Film is used mainly for documentaries and for some dramas shot on location. Endless arguments rage about the merits and demerits of either system; this is likely to add to the confusion of aspiring entrants to the industry, for although an increasing number of technicians move from one technique to the other and back again, there is no doubt that the area in which you first start working can be a decisive factor later on, for it is unfortunately true that a great many people in film and television develop a preference for the technique in which they originally trained.

Incidentally, the term 'Independent' needs clarification nowadays. When commercial television started in Britain, the companies who provided programmes for the different regions (Granada for the north of England, Anglia for the east and so on) called themselves 'Commercial Television Contractors', eventually changing this to 'Independent Television Companies' which led to confusion with the advent of Channel Four. This network produces virtually no programmes itself but acts merely as a publisher, commissioning programmes from either the ITV companies (the former Commercial Television Contractors) or the new breed of independent producers, many of whom left 'Independent Television' or the BBC to set up companies expressly for the purpose of supplying programmes for Channel Four. Many of these have found that the volume of work coming from Channel Four is not sufficient to provide them with a living, so they have overflowed into the production of sponsored or corporate films and videos. Similarly, those independents already working in this area have been successful in getting programme commissions from Channel Four. All that this means for aspiring newcomers is that they should be in no doubt as to which type of 'Independent' they are aiming at – there is considerably less formality involved in the smaller independent production companies than the 'Independent Television Companies'.

6 Video production

The last few years have seen a huge increase in the volume of video production. Some of the new companies involved have their own equipment with attendant permanent staff, but many of them rely on hiring equipment and facilities from a growing number of facilities companies. Such facilities companies may operate with a nucleus of permanent staff but, like the production companies, they also rely on the employment of freelance technicians. These companies may be the independents referred to in section 5 above, they may be concerned solely with corporate, sponsored or business programmes, or they may be 'in-house' units owned by banks, finanancial institutions or conglomerates such as Shell International.

7 Workshops

There are numerous film and video workshops throughout the country which are now recognised by the ACTT (Association of Cinematograph, Television and Allied Technicians) and which operate as production units on a non-profit distributing basis. They are also involved in a range of other activities such as distribution, education and exhibition.

Workshops generally undertake work of a radical nature, addressed to audiences from oppressed and marginalised groups such as young people, working-class communities, women and black people. If your interest lies within these areas, it might be possible to obtain employment with a workshop in a non-technical job and later to work your way into a trainee position on production, which would then lead to the possibility of applying for an ACTT ticket. You can find a list of workshops in the *BFI Film and Television Yearbook.*

Workshops such as Retake Film and Video Collective (the first Asian group to be recognised by the ACTT) run training courses both for beginners and for those with some knowledge of, for instance, 16mm. cameras. There is also now an Association of Black Workshops located at Unit 215, Highbury Workshops, 22 Highbury Grove, London N5 2EA.

2
Anatomy of a Documentary Film Production

The next three chapters provide outline descriptions of the processes involved in the making of different kinds of films and television productions, in order to clarify the nature of the different jobs involved. This chapter deals with the production of a sponsored documentary film (this being the area in which I am experienced), but the various stages are roughly comparable whether the film is for television, video cassette, cinema exhibition or other types of distribution. And indeed most of the description is equally applicable to the production of a feature film; the major differences being, obviously, those of scale, and the use of actors and sets.

The Initial Idea and Briefing

This might come either from the sponsor or from the creative or production side. The initial contact is therefore that made between the sponsor, who is going to provide financial backing, and the producer. At this point the purpose of the film, the target audience and possibly the overall budget for production are discussed. Suitable researchers, script writers and directors are also considered; in the case of documentaries, these three roles may well be undertaken by the same person. It may be that a clear idea of the shape of the film is emerging already, but often the researcher/writer/director must spend some time investigating the subject before proposing the style and length of the film. Following the initial briefing, there is a meeting between the producer, the researcher/writer and technical adviser (if the subject calls for one) in which the general content, level of the audience and overall approach are decided. It is then more or less up to the researcher to find out everything about the subject from those involved in it, with the aim of obtaining as wide a spectrum of views, suggestions and advice as possible. After a week or two of digesting, sifting, eliminating and organising information, the researcher/writer should then be in a position to produce a *treatment*. If one were to be given the task of viewing a film and then to write a description of it from beginning to end in the most visual style possible, the resulting document would be a treatment. The difference at this stage is that the film has not yet been made and is therefore still in the writer's imagination.

During this period, the scriptwriter often consults with the producer to explore various ideas. It is possible that the producer has a greater knowledge both of the sponsor's requirements and of potential political pitfalls, and experienced producers even at this stage may be aware of overall costs and may sometimes have to curb the writer's more outlandish ideas if these are liable to push the production a long way over budget.

The treatment, after being delivered by the writer to the producer, is checked for technical accuracy by the technical adviser and then presented to the sponsor. Inevitably it must be passed round to any other interested parties, and a meeting is called to hear their comments and views. Both the writer and producer are often faced with the task of defending their proposals strongly and firmly.

Assuming that the treatment has been favourably received, the next stage is its development into a shooting script. If the film's director has not written the treatment, this may well be the point at which the director takes over since, in documentaries, most directors choose to write their own shooting scripts.

The shooting script is a detailed, technical document describing each scene numerically with its appropriate action, dialogue and commentary. It is generally laid out in two columns with the visual information on the left and the sound on the right. More detailed research is required at this stage so that a vague description, such as that of 'a village street' will become 'Exterior, the High Street' of a specific location which has been surveyed and deemed suitable.

When the shooting script has been completed, a breakdown of all scenes is made from it, dividing them into Studio Interiors, Location Interiors, Exteriors, listing the actors and facilities required and grouping everything into the beginnings of a shooting schedule which will also make sense geographically if there is a variety of widely spread locations. Depending on the length and complexity of the film, this can be a very complicated jig-saw to fit together; in the case of documentary there is often the additional complication of obtaining the good will of owners of premises, and of filming at times that are convenient to them.

Involved at this stage are the director, production manager and, if there are complicated location lighting requirements, the camera-person and possibly an electrician. With the script breakdown and shooting schedule completed, it is possible to prepare a production budget. This is usually done by the production manager in consultation with the director and producer, along with an accountant. This is the time when problems can surface and conflicts occur. Inevitably the budget comes out higher than anticipated, so some kind of surgery is needed. Can the schedule be shortened? Not according to the director. Can sequences be lost from the script or can they be simplified? Perhaps. Can the number of locations be reduced to cut down travelling time? Can the whole film be shot exterior on Clapham Common? With some squeezing here, some compromise there and perhaps a bit of luck, such as the use of a house as a location in exchange for the price of a good dinner, the package of the agreed shooting script, the breakdown, schedule and production budget can be presented to the sponsor. It is to be hoped that a contract may now be signed, enabling arrangements to be finalised and technicians hired.

Production

Final preparations are now made for the start of the actual production. The production manager has now been joined by the unit manager/ assistant director and they make all practical arrangements such as transport and hotel accommodation (if the film is to be made on location) and issue a movement order and call sheet for the production crew, artists and equipment on Day One.

Let us assume that the film is a fairly simple sponsored industrial documentary to be made on location. The unit would consist in the first place of the director, who is responsible for the planning and creative content of each scene. The cameraperson, in consultation with the director, fixes the actual camera position, camera movement and choice of lens for each shot and is responsible for the quality of the photography. In a documentary, he/she invariably also operates the camera, actually following the action through the viewfinder. With larger studio cameras for feature films or television drama on film, this job is done by a camera operator and the importance of this technician should not be underestimated. His or her experience, both technical and artistic, can be very helpful to the director in the finer points of choosing a set-up, planning moves of actors in relation to the camera, and ensuring that the angles and eyelines are correct in relation to previous or following shots, thus assisting the film editor when he or she comes to make the smoothest and most effective cuts. The cameraperson is also of course responsible for the lighting of each scene and the correct exposure, and is ultimately responsible for every aspect of the photography but has under him or her a camera crew varying from one to three or four assistants. In the case of our imaginary documentary the single assistant is responsible for loading the camera, the correct focus, perhaps operating the zoom, dealing with the clapper board and finally unloading the film and filling in negative report sheets giving particulars of the scenes, type of stock and so on to guide the laboratory doing the developing and printing. In a studio production, these jobs are shared by the larger camera crew and the cameraperson is elevated to the grander title of Lighting cameraperson or even Director of Photography. The crew would now include an operator and a focus puller (whose job is not as simple as one might suppose; with complicated scenes involving elaborate camera movement and moves by actors, constant change of focus is often required, and this has to be accurate and unobtrusive unless some deliberate shock technique is involved).

The fourth member of a camera crew is the clapper/loader, once known as clapper boy, whose clapper-board has become part of the iconography of sound film production. (Sad to report, cameras are now coming into use in which the marking of audible and visible signs to identify the start of the sound and picture will be done electronically inside the camera.) Finally, in a studio production the camera crew will have a grip, whose job is to operate the dolly for tracking shots and to assemble and dismantle the heavy and complicated camera equipment with its attendant forms of mount.

Next in this modest documentary unit there will be the sound crew, consisting of a sound recordist who operates a portable ¼″ tape recorder pulsed to record synchronously with the camera, and a boom swinger or operator who is responsible for the microphone being in the best position to record the highest quality sound at all times whilst ensuring that neither the microphone nor its shadow intrude into the picture area. If only synchronised sound effects and background dialogue are to be recorded, these two jobs can be done by one person in a documentary production, but in larger and more complicated productions the number of sound crew can increase to three or four, one of whom has the sole responsibility for ensuring that the equipment is serviceable.

Finally on the production side, there is the unit manager/assistant director. This is a very important and responsible job on documentaries, especially as the person who fills that post is not only responsible for the smooth running of the show and for the contentment of all the technicians but also for ensuring that the production keeps to schedule, the practical arrangements are organised and everything and everybody required for each shot is there at the appointed place and time. These tasks often require the utmost charm, tact and persuasiveness; in most documentaries, the goodwill and often practical involvement of amateurs, owners of premises and even casual passers by is sought. Most such people are, in my experience, extremely tolerant, but often the whole process is far more complicated and takes much longer than they imagine and their patience can be sorely tried. It is here as well that the presence of producers can be helpful if they are prepared to act as unofficial public relations officers, persuading volunteers of the value of their contributions and of the projected usefulness of the finished film. This task is certainly made easier if the film is to be of an educational nature or is sponsored for some charitable cause.

The unit manager is also responsible for money, paying out for facilities, paying for technicians' meals and hotels. All in all, even if only engaged on a freelance basis on one particular film, the unit manager should be regarded as an 'agent of the company', keeping all the wheels well-oiled and safeguarding the budget against the sometimes over-zealous whims of the unit's creative personnel.

Of course, even in a modest documentary film, more people can be involved: electricians if lights are required on location; an art director, a casting director, carpenters, painters and prop people to build a set if necessary or adapt and dress an existing location; make-up, hairdressing or wardrobe if actors are involved; a continuity person (now called a script supervisor) if the production is for cinema or television or is a complex documentary; catering staff if the location is far from civilisation or if large numbers are involved. All this in turn can lead to additional assistant directors being employed to assist in the organisation. In larger productions, third assistant directors may be no more than glorified call-persons, tea organisers and runners rolled into one.

So the days and weeks of the production schedule go on and, bit by bit, the film is nearer to reaching the next stage – Editing.

Editing

Usually at the end of each day's shooting, the camera assistant or clapper/loader unloads the exposed film and fills in the negative report sheets giving all the particulars of the production: scene numbers and footage, together with instructions to the film processing laboratory for developing and printing. The cans are taken to the laboratory or picked up by it from a pre-arranged point and, provided they reach the processing plant by about midnight, they can be developed and printed by early the following morning. Those accustomed to working in video find even this delay intolerable, but it is a system which usually works fairly well. The unit, if it is still on location, telephones the contact man at the laboratory and gets a report on the rushes. This term, which has prevailed over the years, indicates a sense of urgency in the proceedings; still necessary if there is any question of problems arising out of the previous day's shooting which would call for re-takes. In feature films, this might extend to holding highly paid actors for additional days or not striking a particular set to make way for another, all of which can play havoc with a schedule and budget.

But, assuming the report on the rushes is satisfactory, prints of all the selected scenes shot the previous day are despatched to the production company's offices or wherever the cutting or editing room is located for this particular production. In parallel with this, at the end of the day's shooting the sound crew will have despatched the ¼" tape recorded to a department of a sound studio equipped for transferring ¼" tape to the appropriate gauge, 16mm. or 35mm. of sprocketed magnetic tape. This is also delivered to the cutting room as quickly as possible. The master ¼" may also be returned for storage in the cutting room but the film negative remains stored and filed away in the laboratory, for the moment merely developed, but otherwise exactly as it came out of the camera. And there it will remain for some time until the final stages of production are reached, of which more anon.

The first job in the cutting room is for the assistant editor to take the picture and sound rushes and synchronise them in rolls ready for viewing. This is where the clapper board comes in, for this is the device used not only for identifying each scene with a number but also for identifying the exact moment when the hinged parts of the board come together with their resultant loud clap. This enables the assistant editor to get the scene in synch and then, by running picture and sound together in a sprocketed machine called a synchroniser, keep them running in parallel throughout the scene. All the scenes are assembled with appropriate lengths of blank film or spacing in between so that the rushes can be viewed by the director, editor, cameraperson, sound recordist and producer as soon as possible. If the unit is working at a nearby location or in a studio then the rushes will be viewed at lunch time or in the evening in a convenient viewing theatre. Mobile projectors may also be taken to the location, or a nearby cinema may be booked for the screening.

Attitudes vary as to whether an entire unit should attend a rushes viewing. If the producer and director have no objection, then being able to see material in the raw and to hear immediate comments is valuable training for the newcomer such as a third assistant director.

16

The assistant projectionist in a production viewing theatre (not an ordinary public cinema) can gain the same experience whilst at the same time learning how to handle film and the technical jargon involved. This is then a step nearer to obtaining work in a cutting room or in the camera department.

The rushes are viewed day by day and if, for any reason such as the remoteness of the location or the tightness of the shooting schedule, the director is not watching them regularly, then the producer and editor will report fully and make constructive comments.

After viewing, the picture and sound will be sent for numbering – that is, the printing of the scene number and the cumulative footage (from the clapper board to where the camera has cut), down the side of the film so that, however the scene is subsequently edited, the picture and the magnetic sound can be put into a synchroniser and kept in synch. Studios operate their own numbering machines with operators and there are companies that exist specifically to provide this service. The job of 'numbering boy', whilst not particularly creative in itself, is again a good introduction to the industry.

After numbering, the assistant editor will log all the rushes in a notebook, writing the scene numbers with an appropriate short description for each, the edge numbers which are printed by the stock manufacturers, and the new 'rubber' numbers which have just been printed. This is a laborious but essential task which the newcomer takes an enormous time to complete but which, with practice, can be done quite speedily. If by this time the rushes have been viewed by all concerned, the assistant editor 'breaks down' the rolls into individual scenes, wrapping and labelling each separately; it is here that the assistant's responsibility really begins, for upon a neat filing system depends the subsequent continuous putting away and getting out of all the material which is part of the normal editing process of cutting scenes together – shortening one, lengthening another, trying a cut this way and that way. The ability of the assistant to file away and find again quickly even a few frames of film is essential to the editor.

It may now be possible, even whilst the film is still being shot, for the assistant editor to start assembling the scenes, still in their individual little rolls, together in script order for the editor to start work. The editor starts to assemble the cutting copy of reel one of our film and now there may be glimmerings of the final result. It may be, however, that the director will prefer to watch all the material again with the editor before he starts cutting, in which case the assistant editor would not have 'broken down the rushes'.

But assuming the editor has started work and by now has all the material to hand, enabling him to assemble the cutting copy of the film into a first rough cut, he or she will screen it for the director, who inevitably will have views on what could be changed, shortened, dispensed with and so on. Invariably the running time of the film is longer than intended and so, very often, agonising decisions have to be made as to what should be cut out: it is here that a good editor's objective view can be useful. The director may tend still to cherish certain sequences or even individual scenes, remembering perhaps the difficulties of achieving them, but the editor is more able to consider the clarity, pace and effectiveness of the film as a whole. Proposed surgery may seem callous but experience and talent in this area should be heeded by the director.

Eventually the director and editor will be more or less satisfied with the state of the rough cut. In the case of our original imaginary documentary, it might be that one of them has recorded a rough or 'scratch' commentary, perhaps in the cutting room on a cassette tape recorder, and this is transferred to sprocketed magnetic tape and fitted to synchronise with the picture, helping to set the general pace of the whole film. This will now be screened for the producer and, provided he or she is satisfied that the film not only works as film but also fulfills the original sponsors brief, a showing is arranged for the sponsor.

This, at times, can be a very trying experience. Much as the producer does his or her best to discourage it, the sponsor is tempted to pack the viewing theatre with experts, superiors and other assorted interested parties. Of course, those providing the financial backing should be given an opportunity to see the film at this stage while it is still possible to make changes, but it has to be admitted that a rough cut with perhaps a 'scratch' commentary, only a few natural sound effects, no titles, no music and the footage perhaps scratched from harsh treatment in the cutting room, needs a lot of faith on the part of non-professional viewers for them to foresee that the finished product will indeed be the magnificent production that everybody has hoped for. In the case of a rough cut showing of a sponsored film, the audience usually waits at the end of the screening to observe the reactions of the top person present; the pause whilst waiting for his comments can seem to stretch to eternity. But in the case of our imaginary film, let's be optimistic and say that the 'Chairman' is delighted: everyone else then invariably echoes his pleasure. We are therefore ready to move to the next stage, preparing the film for final recording and dubbing. At this stage with larger productions, the film may gradually pass to a dubbing editor who, with assistants, starts assembling all the sound tracks, recording or obtaining from a library suitable sound effects, laying music tracks and so on. But we shall stick to our simple documentary to follow through the next stage of production.

If there is a commentary, a suitable voice has to be chosen and recorded, either 'to picture', with the recording being made in a sound proof booth while the commentator watches the film projected and is cued when to start and stop, or the recording can be 'wild', that is, without running the picture but merely in a soundproof studio. In this latter case, the director and editor, who attend the recording session, will have to know whether there are any sections of the film where the recording requires careful timing. The 'recording to picture' method does not require this but does call for greater experience on the part of the commentator, and some people therefore maintain that it is possible to get a more relaxed performance if the recording is 'wild'.

The assistant editor will also attend the recording session and note the preferred 'takes' of each section or even of each sentence where there is a choice. The recording itself is made by a sound recordist or engineer and, after completion, the tape will again be transferred to sprocketed tape and taken to the cutting room to be synchronised with the picture on a separate roll. So by now each reel of the film may consist of three or more rolls: the action cutting copy, the dialogue, and now the commentary.

By now the director and editor will be thinking about the final planning of the rest of the soundtrack: where music is required and whether any extra sound effects are needed to enhance natural sound and make some additional dramatic point. Once music sections have been decided upon, if the music is to be specially composed then each scene is measured precisely and given to the composer after he or she has watched the film with the editor, director and producer. The general style of the music is discussed, along with the number and type of musicians: anything from a single harmonica to a symphony orchestra. The size of the budget is a factor but, even if money is no object, a symphony orchestra may not necessarily prove the most effective means of adding to the impact of a film.

If library music is to be used, then the editor and director start on a laborious search to find suitable recordings. In the case of specially composed music, however, it is not until arrival at the music recording studio, with the musicians assembled and the film projected with the accompanying music, that one hears for the first time what the composer has come up with. It has been known for the producer, director and editor to realise that they have a disaster on their hands and to have to chuck it all away and go back to the record library. The increasing use of electronically produced music helps, as it is possible for the composer to make changes throughout.

The music recording studio is manned by a recording engineer; most composers have their favourite engineers who they feel do justice to their work. Other jobs involved at this stage include sound recordists, who are monitoring and recording on to the tape, and projectionists, who are screening the film; the conductor, who also may often be the composer, usually conducts each section of music 'to picture', facing the screen so that, if necessary, the tempo can be varied slightly to ensure that the music fits exactly. For a newcomer with leanings towards very high quality sound recording, any job in a music recording studio could be recommended. Unfortunately, with the growth of the 'pop' recording industry, the number of people with the ambition to record music has grown enormously and so studios find themselves inundated with job applications.

Once the music has been recorded, the ¼" tape is once again transferred to sprocketed tape and another roll is synchronised in the cutting room and added to the existing collection. The additional sound effects are now added and may either be inserted in the spaces in the music roll or further rolls may be constructed. The synchroniser is now being used to the full, accommodating not only the picture, the action cutting copy, but also up to three other rolls running synchronously. Once again, the assistant editor needs to be a tidy and methodical sort of super-librarian, knowing where each sound effect, each spare take of music and so on can be found in the mounting crescendo of work that normally accompanies a film approaching the stage when it will be ready for dubbing. The final task is to prepare the dubbing cue sheet, a giant chart which acts as a guide to the recordist, in this case a specialist called a dubbing mixer, and which should give exact footages and descriptions where anything happens that has bearing on the final mixed or dubbed track. The dubbing theatre is a recording studio where it is possible to run all the sound tracks (the number of which might by now have risen to five or six) synchronously with the picture, forwards or backwards. Some dubbing theatres can accommodate as many as ten tracks. The task of the dubbing mixer is to watch the picture, consult the cue sheet and to mix and record all these separate tracks into one master with each sound at the correct level to give maximum dramatic impact without drowning out dialogue or commentary, and avoiding such a babble of sound that the whole film becomes confused and fussy. This is an extremely skilled job and can also be highly creative. The entire dubbing operation is one of co-operation between the mixer, the editor and the director and producer, all of whom usually attend the session, for in all probability only now will the entire sound track of the film be heard by all concerned, and sometimes some cherished theories concocted in the cutting room may turn out untenable.

Gradually, by reviewing the film in stages, moving forward and back again or 'rocking and rolling' and pre-mixing one section and then returning to add some other sounds, the final mixed or dubbed track is recorded. As in the music recording studio, the mixer in the dubbing theatre is supported by other recordists and assistants and a larger number of projectionists to cope with the lacing and unlacing of the quantity of separate tracks in the specially designed projection box.

The film is now almost ready for its final stage in the laboratory. It may be, however, that a screening of the action cutting copy and a magnetic copy of the mixed track is called for, and, during the run-up to dubbing, the matter of optical effects (that is fades, dissolves and so on) will also have been organised with the laboratory. There is also the question of titles. These can vary from a simple card at the front of the film to elaborate affairs which become mini-productions in their own right. They are usually designed by a graphics artist in consultation with the director and editor, and the artist may be free-lance, work in a department of a laboratory or be part of an animation company. After the titles are made up, they are photographed to the length required on a rostrum camera operated by a cameraperson who specialises in this type of work.

And so all the ingredients of the film are assembled – the action cutting copy with titles and opticals inserted, and the master of the final mixed track – and everything is despatched to the laboratory for the final stages.

Completion

At this stage, the action cutting copy consists of a number of prints from the original negative, cut and joined together with specially strengthened tape. The negative, it should be remembered, has remained at the laboratory untouched, apart from the possibility of it having been logged and broken down in exactly the same way as the assistant editor dealt with the rushes prints soon after they first arrived in the cutting room. The big difference is that we are dealing with the precious original negative of the film, and handling must be carried out in scrupulously clean conditions, with members of the negative department wearing white cotton gloves.

When the cutting copy is received, it is the job of the negative cutter to match each scene of negative to the corresponding print in the cutting copy by means of the edge numbers which appear down the edge of the negative and which have printed through on to the print. Each scene of negative is then joined by a heat welding process to the next and gradually a reel of cut action negative is assembled. In parallel with this, the master magnetic dubbed track has been transferred either at the dubbing theatre or the laboratory to an optical negative which is then developed and sent to the negative cutter to be synchronised with the action cut negative.

Now the cans of action and sound negative containing the precious material, the result of weeks, months or years of sweat, toil and tears of a great many people, are ready to make the first copy of the film. The value and uniqueness of the picture is so great at this stage that often a duplicate negative or intermediate fine grain print (from the negative) may be struck, if only to satisfy the insurance brokers.

There is, however, one important technical job outstanding and that is the grading of each scene by a colour grader to ensure that the finest and most even colour rendering is obtained. The cameraperson may be consulted unless, as so often happens, they are miles away on some new assignment; the editor and director may also be involved, especially if some special effect such as printing for night shots is required.

And so the first graded finished print from the negative of picture and sound is combined to produce an answer or check print. The complexity of the colour printing process means that inevitably some scenes will require changes in grading here and there until everyone is satisfied. In the case of our imaginary sponsored documentary, the producer, director, editor and any other creative personnel who may still be present can now screen the finished results to the sponsor.

3
Anatomy of a Corporate Video Production

The portability and convenience of video cameras, the cheapness of videotape stock, the possibility of rapid editing and quick and economical duplication of videocassette copies are all factors that have led to an enormous increase in the production of what have become know as corporate videos. These are really no different from industrial and business-sponsored films, apart from the general tendency to think that they will cost less: indeed, because of the speed of production and delivery, this may be the case, because they are often made for a specific short-term purpose and may therefore become obsolete more rapidly.

How does the growth of this side of the production industry affect would-be entrants? The initial setting up, script writing, scheduling, budgeting and preparation should in theory be exactly the same as for a sponsored documentary film although in practice, due to more modest budgets or greater urgency, some aspects may be skimped and the operation treated more like a television current affairs programme. But whereas in the case of current affairs the overiding factor is to get the programme on the air, the corporate video is representing the views and philosophy of the sponsor, and lack of preparation as far as practical arrangements and script are concerned can lead to enormous misunderstandings during completion. I have touched on this political side of the business only because corporate videos are often made with a much smaller production unit and therefore even the newest assistant/trainee might unwittingly become embroiled.

The smallest production unit for a professional video would consist of a director, video cameraperson and engineer doubling as sound recordist. The proliferation of production companies, especially outside London, means that there may be opportunities for new entrants. But it should be noted that creative and technical standards may not be all that high and the growth in the number of low-budget, small-crewed productions does not help the image of the audio-visual communications industry as a whole.

The employers' organisations and the trade unions should indeed get together to work out a sensible structure for rates, conditions and crewing for the corporate video sector. What this might mean for the aspiring entrant is that the production unit would be increased to include an assistant director or production assistant and, on more elaborate productions, a second assistant or runner, making the structure similar to those of films. The video camera crew will often operate more efficiently with the addition of an engineer and a separate sound recordist, who increasingly may record sound on ¼″ tape in just the same way as in film; and as with film, if elaborate dialogue scenes are involved, a boom operator/assistant sound recordist may be added. Here is another good starting point for those with an interest in sound recording. Anything other than the most rudimentary portable lighting will call, if only in the interests of safety, for one or more qualified electricians who are generally members of the EEPTU.

Another difference in the production of corporate video as opposed to documentary film, especially as far as jobs are concerned, is at the editing and completion stages. The most common practice now is for the programme to be recorded scene by scene with a single camera. The start and finish of each scene of each separate video cassette will be electronically recorded with a time-code, particulars of which will have been noted during production by the engineer. At the end of the day or of the production as a whole, all these rolls of master tape will be transferred to another tape complete with the time-code for 'off-line editing'. The transfer is usually carried out by a facilities company, possibly the same company that has already supplied the camera and recording equipment and which may also be editing the programme. In the larger production companies, some or all of these facilities are 'in house'.

The job of doing the transfers is reasonably routine, though requiring some knowledge of electronics, and so this may be a fruitful area for potential entrants. The copies from the original master tapes now pass to the editor for off-line editing. This is creatively the same as film editing to rough cut stage, but instead of physically cutting film prints the cuts are made electronically by transfer to yet another video cassette. A large amount of re-editing, involving further transfers, results in ever diminishing picture quality so that by the time the rough edit is ready to be shown to the producer and the sponsor the picture may bear scant resemblance to the original master tape and a sponsor will need a lot of reassurance that his final programme will in fact be as good to look at as the original.

Video editors have in many cases been self-taught and have taken advantage of the fact that the actual machinery requires some practice to operate, and this has therefore discouraged more conservative film editors from learning the ropes in the video editing suite. More and more film editors are nevertheless crossing the divide into video, thus bringing their creative skills with them.

The finishing touches to a video are not made until the final or on-line edit, and here another editing skill is required. In the final edit suite adjustments can not only be made to the cut, but titles, captions and all those elaborate electronic effects are added. The speed and resourcefulness required to feed in all the necessary information is staggering. The off-line editor will have taken note or logged all the time-coding of the off-line cut, for at this stage of the 'on-line' the editor will be going back to the original master tapes and creating a new cut master. The director and producer and possibly even the sponsor may all be present during the 'on-line' edit, which may stretch on for hour after weary hour into the night. The late hours seem to be a tradition emanating from the urgency of completing a programme for television transmission or from the feeling of pop video producers that working at night is exciting and stimulating and this seems to permeate the whole video editing business. It is in such situations that a tea-person will prove useful; the worth and opportunities of such an apparently menial job should not be sneered at.

Another stage in the completion of our corporate video is the recording of commentary, music and the addition of more sound effects, all of which have to be laid in and mixed at appropriate levels.

This is exactly equivalent to the process of film recording and mixing, but in the case of video may be completed at the on-line edit. In the case of more elaborate programmes, some recordings may have been done before the on-line and the final dubbing will have to be done afterwards. The job opportunities are, however, precisely the same as for film recording and dubbing.

The final stage of production is the making of video cassette copies from the master. This is normally done by specialised duplicating houses and can be quite an elaborate affair if U-Matics, VHS and Beta copies are all required and on different technical standards for foreign countries. People who operate the duplicating machines, as well as controlling the quality have therefore to be particularly orderly so that the numbers and types required are correct. Finally, cassettes may have to be labelled, put into library cases into which cover flats (comparable to book jackets) have been inserted. This is not the most satisfying of jobs, but it does give a newcomer the chance to handle video cassettes and observe the technicalities of duplication, which in turn is a step towards becoming a video tape operator/engineer in an edit suite or a television or video studio.

To sum up, therefore, job opportunities in the video side of the industry may be improved if the applicant has knowledge and qualifications in electronics but, as with film, 'hands on' experience of the equipment may be just as useful. Creative aspects of video should be precisely the same as film; that is, good scripting and story telling, with additional knowledge of the technical innovations which electronic wizardry can provide almost instantaneously, including a wealth of video effects and computer animation. It should be remembered that virtually every effect that has become commonplace on video can be achieved optically on film but at a cost of considerably more time and money.

4

Anatomy of a Television Production

Here is an outline of the procedure for producing a studio-based play to be recorded on video tape for television.

Having bought a script or hired a writer, the producer then looks for a director. Some producers are also directors, but in the case of a play or series of plays different directors are normally assigned to each programme. The director sets up an office with a production assistant or secretary for the production. It is from here that the creation, administration and organisation of the particular programme takes place. At this stage the hierarchy is clear – the director works for the producer and everyone else works for the director. The writer also works for the director, sometimes through a script editor, who is engaged on a series on which different writers are working, so that the overall style is co-ordinated.

Several operations are now run in parallel. These are mainly matters of selecting the production crew and scheduling the production, but the selected personnel may still be engaged in other work and therefore are not involved at this early stage. The director meanwhile works with the casting department to choose the actors who will play the various parts. The producer will also be involved in this operation, especially if the production is a series rather than a one-off programme.

The production assistant (working for the director) is organising facilities and other matters as required. A stage manager is appointed to join the director. Rehearsals begin with a read through, usually in a big room in which the stage manager has marked the floor to indicate the ground plan of the various sets. Prior to this, the director and stage manager will have been working with the designer and the design department and, as well as a ground plan, there is often a model of the studio lay-out available. This helps the actors and the director to visualise the shots and set-ups of the final production.

Outside location filming or video shooting has by now been organised and all other departments such as wardrobe and make-up are now assigned to the production. Scenery is being built, while properties are made, bought, hired or withdrawn from stock.

By now the studio and all its 'in house' facilities will have been allocated. The various crews for camera, sound, scenery, lighting and all the rest are now scheduled. These would normally consist of permanent staff employed by the television company, but might include some free-lancers. In the case of a production made by an independent company, most of the people in creative posts may be freelance.

The director has now written his camera script and various planning meetings are held, followed by a technical rehearsal. This takes place in the rehearsal room and is for the benefit of the technicians, all of whom will now have a copy of the camera script. At each stage of the production, difficulties are discussed and ironed out or last-minute changes or suggestions are made or adaptions to the script agreed to.

By Day One in the studio everything has been scheduled, including practical considerations such as lunch breaks. The scenery, props and lighting are usually set up before the actors and director start work, although adjustments are being made all the time.

Unlike traditional filming, where the director stays near the camera on the studio floor, in a video production the director is in a control room with screens monitoring what each camera is picking up. During the shooting of a scene, the director instructs the vision mixer to make the cut from one camera to another; experienced vision mixers reach the stage of virtually being able to anticipate the director's orders, especially if the sequence of camera moves has been well rehearsed. The director is in direct radio link with the floor manager, camera crews and other studio technicians.

The director then begins what is sometimes called the 'stagger'. Each shot or sequence of shots in a scene is rehearsed with all technical facilities, cameras, sound, special effects etc., until perfect. If the shooting is to be carried out on a 'rehearse record' basis, like a film set, then that scene or sequence is shot and recorded. Nowadays most television plays are shot in chunks, sometimes out of script order. It is rare for a long scene or part of a play to be shot from beginning to end and the studio days are now taken up with several 'rehearse record' set ups.

This process has necessitated changes in recording techniques, and time code numbers are used to facilitate editing the programme together after the days in the studio. The production assistant places an electronic coding on to the tape and logs each shot or piece of recording so that it can easily be located. The coding usually consists of six figures indicating the exact time (in hours, minutes and seconds) that the recording was made.

Editing video tape is becoming more and more like film editing, the major difference being that the machinery used for video is electronically based and the VTR editor can only see the pictures on a monitor screen, albeit frame by frame, whereas the film editor can see the photographic images on the film itself, in addition to being able to screen them on a miniature screen. The two techniques might be compared to a pilot flying a light aircraft as opposed to flying a jumbo jet. It is a question of knowing the intricacies of the equipment.

After editing there is still sound dubbing to be completed: adding effects or voices and music. This is virtually the same technique as film dubbing and uses the same grades of technicians.

5
Starting Points

Let us consider a number of routes that might be taken towards employment on specific jobs within the industry. Most of the people I have interviewed, when questioned about their ultimate ambitions, simply reply that they want to *direct*. What, then is their best starting point, irrespective of qualifications and experience?

As a general rule the best way of getting a specific job in any of the creative posts, editing, sound recording, design, animation and so on, is to seek employment as a trainee on the lowliest position in that particular department. Employment in secretarial, accountancy, office junior and tea-making capacities can also be an effective way of entering the organisational and administrative grades within the industry, and those engaged in such posts have been known to move up to more creative positions.

But, the best method to study the technique and style of established film directors is via the editing department. There could not be a better start to any career in the film industry than a job as a trainee assistant editor in the cutting room. The career path could then lead from a post as assistant editor to that of editor and thence to a chance to direct anything from the most modest pick-up shots or inserts to 'second unit' shooting on a feature film.

In the case of television production on video, a more frequent starting point is employment in a modest studio production job, progressing through floor management and perhaps vision-mixing to direction. The post of vision-mixer has by tradition been female-dominated and so the upward route there has tended to originate in the use of secretarial skills. Equal opportunity laws could eventually balance the numbers of men and women in senior creative and administrative positions in the industry. At the moment there are many more men in such posts, but there are few jobs in each department and at any level in which no women are employed. Camera operation, both on film and video, is where one would be hard pushed to find many women working (unlike in the USA and the USSR). The usual reason given is the bulkiness of the equipment, but future trends towards miniaturisation may herald changes here as well.

Another possible route for the aspiring director is via script writing and research. But first, how does one become a script writer? In the case of feature films and television drama, the way lies in writing a story suitable for adaptation and, if this is taken up, as an option, in pursuing one's rights as the author to collaborate on the subsequent adaptation with either an experienced script writer or the director. This is where film school graduates have an advantage in that they may possibly be provided with more opportunities to write an original script.

The writing of an outline script for a sponsored documentary might well impress a potential employer; if you could attract prior interest from a sponsor (either through personal contacts or by sheer perseverence), you would stand a good chance of being engaged on the project by a documentary producer. As an example, I was once approached by an Australian writer with an idea for a film about heraldry; the initial concept was attractive and made doubly so when he told me there was interest and the chance of financial backing from an industrial company who were to have a Grant of Arms in their centenary year. I suggested a liaison between the company and the British Tourist Authority, and the result was a successful co-production on heraldry set in the context of British tradition and heritage. A further example was the writer who approached me with a newspaper article about the dangers of working on off-shore oil rigs, and proposed a series of safety films. I in turn approached an oil company and the films were duly made.

A continuing involvement in the writing of scripts for documentary films may well lead to the chance to direct, if only because the subject may be so specialised that the writer becomes the only person in possession of the requisite knowledge of that subject.

From time to time, jobs as researchers in television documentaries become available. New entrants will have a better chance of being taken on by a company if they are able to demonstrate a specialised knowledge of the subject under research. This in turn can lead to script writing and, ultimately, to directing.

Those with ambitions towards becoming film camerapersons start out as camera assistants; the most junior grade in this category is clapper/loader. Although these are still often referred to as clapper *boys*, it is said that in Hollywood some have stayed in this post until retirement age; it is true that the amount of money that can be earned (with overtime) in all the camera assistant grades is considerable and lessens the incentive for promotion. In some instances, documentary camerapersons have become directors and on occasion, feature camerapersons have become feature directors but, on the whole, the art of achieving good photographic results and the excitement of new developments in cameras and lenses is sufficiently satisfying and rewarding for most. A feasible method of introduction into the camera department is through companies that specialise in hiring out camera equipment.

The role of the producer, along with that of the director, is the most responsible job in films and television. The producer is in overall charge of any production and therefore initially assembles the components of the entire project, selecting the principal creative people, finding the money, or (if the money is already found) taking ultimate responsibility for the budget.

Although the director is responsible for the creative content of the production, the producer must see to it that the budget or schedule is adhered to or that excess in either area can be justified. He has also to keep backers and sponsors happy, if necessary preventing them from interfering in the shooting, or reassuring them if some of the creative processes appear wild and extravagant. He is ultimately responsible for keeping a unit working in harmony during production and, on the creative side, must be ready to advise and influence the whole project with the utmost tact. Some directors believe that producers are an unnecessary incumbrance and, indeed, there are many successful producer/directors. Nevertheless, many directors are glad to be relieved of the organisational and entrepreneurial roles and appreciate that the slightly more detached viewpoint of the producer can, at its best, be beneficial and helpful.

How does one set about becoming a producer? One method is, of course, by progressing gradually through the various ranks of technical jobs, including perhaps directing, and by finally taking on the dual role of producer/director on a personal project. Equally there are many people who would say with some cynicism that producers need to have had no practical experience of technical production: all that is required of them is an idea, some flair, business acumen, access to money and the ambition to be the 'Captain of the Ship'.

6

Looking for a Job

So how does one set about looking for a job? The first step is to obtain copies of all the trade directories; these are available in the reference departments of the public libraries. The most comprehensive of them, by far, is *Kemp's Film and TV Directory;* other titles include *Contacts* (published by *Spotlight Casting Directory*), *Screen International Film and TV Yearbook, Electro-Media,* and the *BFI Film and Television Yearbook. The Knowledge* is the latest and biggest directory of individual technicians, facilities and so on, with a listing of some 350 companies and a host of other information, but it is addressed primarily to people already in the film industry. It is expensive (£50 in 1989, £35 to accredited film students) but copies are available in public libraries.

After selecting the broad area in which you want to work (Feature, Documentaries, Television, Animation, etc.) you should make a list of the companies which are currently active. Then compose a suitable letter. This should be short and to the point, neatly handwritten or (preferably) typed. It is a good idea to find out the name of somebody influential at each company and write to him or her; otherwise write to the Managing Director. In the case of the BBC and Independent Television Companies, write to the Personnel Officer and ask for a job application form. Be prepared to write up to two hundred letters but resist the temptation to photocopy them, although you may attach a photocopy of your curriculum vitae. Expect very little response but do not lose heart. Contact any companies that have acknowledged your letter, perhaps even some of those who haven't, and enquire if there is anyone prepared to give you advice. If you are successful in getting an appointment, seek help and suggestions of other names and companies you might contact. On the whole, people who work in films or television are informal and friendly and if you succeed in making contact with one or two sympathetic people, whether in senior positions, secretarial posts or traineeships try to maintain these contacts. Most people will not begrudge telling you about their particular jobs and are often prepared to show you what their work entails. But do avoid pestering people, especially if they are heavily immersed in a project with a deadline to meet.

What in your initial letter and in any subsequent interview is likely to attract a potential employer? Academic achievements are important, of course, especially to the BBC and Independent Television Companies, where there is heavy competition for jobs. But there can be additional elements that contribute to an even more attractive package. Obviously potential script writers should try to phrase their letters in a pungent and witty style. I once engaged someone purely as a result of an exceptionally well-written letter (he is now the Head of Films at one of the larger Independent Television Companies).

Membership of film societies or amateur film groups may convince potential employers of a continuing interest in production techniques. And nowadays home video recording may be a spur to experimentation in DIY television production at home. Certainly, admitting to an interest in photography and ownership of a Super-8 movie camera can never be a drawback to the aspiring cameraperson; making amateur movies, however outrageous and hamfisted, may indicate that a desire to become a professional film-maker is no passing whim. Be prepared to travel if it is at all possible. Jobs may be available outside London, both in television companies and companies specialising in documentaries and commercials.

If, in spite of all your efforts, you find yourself out of luck, you might consider looking at peripheral activities with a view to transferring at a later date to the film and television industries proper. These include:

1. Slide/Tape and multi-media productions, in which many of the techniques, especially on the soundtrack, are comparable to those of film.
2. Radio commercials, where recording is akin to the processes used in film and television.

3. Advertising agencies with television and radio departments, where you might come into contact with people who are engaged in productions for the agency on a sub-contractual basis.

4. In-house photographic, film and video production in other industries, where standards can be every bit as high as in commercial production companies.

5. Theatre; in the provinces in particular, there may be links with local television companies. But it should be noted that competition for jobs in this area is as heavy as for films and television.

6. Film processing laboratories; this used to be a well-known stepping stone to a job in production but employers are now more wary about taking on those who are obviously regarding it as short-term employment.

7. Educational television; those with experience of teaching and who want to move into production may find this a particularly good starting point.

The actual job-seeking process demands time, persistence and money. But in spite of the haphazard methods of entry, year by year the industry *does* admit newcomers, so it is worth persevering.

7

Joining the BBC

For the last thirty years or so, anyone trying to get a job in the film industry or in Independent Television soon discovered that non-membership of a trade union appeared to be an insuperable barrier. A Catch-22 situation seemed to prevail: no job without a union ticket, and no union ticket without a job. Officially, the Association of Cinematograph and Television Technicians (ACTT) has never operated a closed shop, although this was true of the Broadcast and Entertainment Trades Alliance (BETA). But few employers would have considered hiring non-union people on the production side unless they were satisfied that no suitable union member was available.

But there is now a change in this situation. New government legislation concerning trade unions means that no one can be prevented from applying and being accepted for a job on the ground of non-membership of a union. No employee can be prevented from applying subsequently for membership of a union, and the union ticket is still something to be highly recommended. For, as in other industries, so in the film industry, it was the tremendous exploitation of workers that led to the founding of unions in the first place. Indeed, there are still unscrupulous and shady employers in both film and television, making the protection and vigilance of trades unions as necessary as ever. Broadly speaking, a high percentage of people in film and television are still free-lance, and for much of the time there are more people available than jobs. This has led, understandably, to feelings of resentment when trained technicians who are members of a union are passed over in favour of a non-union member who might even be a friend or a relation of the employer.

When the new legislation is really up and running, it remains to be seen whether the employment of inexperienced non-union people might be sufficiently galling to the rest of the production team to provoke them into some kind of protest.

So what does all this mean to an aspiring entrant? It means that, more than ever, you have got to convince potential employers that your enthusiasm, knowledge, training (if you have any), talent and willingness to start in any position, however lowly, will make you a real asset to the project or company. In the days when membership of a trade union was a prerequisite for a job, there were two ways round the problem: the first was to enroll in one of the establishments offering formal training and recognised by the ACTT, and the second was to join the BBC.

Undoubtedly, the finest start to any career in television is still the BBC. But because their charter decrees that all vacancies shall be advertised, the competition for new entrants is extremely keen, and they can afford to be very selective. Vacancies are advertised in the *Listener,* some national newspapers, specialist trade journals like *Screen International* and, in the case of regional vacancies, provincial papers.

Here are some of the categories in which vacancies may occur:

1 Production Appointments

The majority of these vacancies are filled through internal competition, but some posts may be available to outside applicants. For work in Drama and Light Entertainment, almost all production staff are recruited at the level of floor assistant or assistant floor manager (similar to call-boy and assistant stage manager in the theatre). These jobs are often holiday relief work on a short contract, but this could lead to a permanent post. Candidates must be over 21 and have experience back-stage in the professional theatre.

For work on factual programmes in Current Affairs, Features, Documentary or Outside Broadcasts, experience in professional journalism or film-making is the main qualification. In specialist areas, a particular aptitude or qualification, say in science, music, sport or the arts, would also be needed. Production posts in Educational Broadcasting would obviously require experience in teaching or a related field.

Assistant producers' work carries a good deal of responsibility and may involve some studio or film direction, and therefore vacancies are invariably recruited from within the BBC or from other professional television sources, but a knowledge of television techniques and, in the case of factual or educational programmes, a record of professional journalism or teaching, *might* be an attraction should a vacancy arise.

Researchers, again, are normally recruited from the BBC's own staff, but if you specialise in one particular area or subject you could be considered for employment.

Production assistants are normally promoted from production secretaries already working in the BBC, and the job demands first-class secretarial skills plus the ability to work for long hours under pressure and deal with a wide variety of contacts while working in a small production team.

2 Film Training

Film still plays a major role in television production and the BBC's film operation is based at Ealing (in the former Ealing Film Studios). The basic operational unit consists of a cameraperson and assistant, sound recordist and assistant, a lighting electrician and, later in the cutting room, a film editor and assistant, backed up by a film assistant who operates projectors in preview and dubbing theatres. Many an eminent editor started their career in this latter job, by the way.

The qualifications required for acceptance as a trainee are that candidates should be at least 18 years old, with O-levels which include physics and/or maths, but more importantly, perhaps, they should prove an *active* interest in films and film-making and be well informed on photography and the cinema, while assistant sound recordists must additionally have an interest in magnetic sound recording and electronics. Training is carried out at Ealing and 'on the job', with additional specialised training for sound recordists.

3 Television Design

a) Design Assistants

Some previous training in architectural or exhibition draughtsmanship is essential since most of the work involves the preparation of working drawings and ground plans to facilitate the production designer's ideas. A degree or equivalent from an art school or polytechnic is a basic necessity, whether it be in interior design, the history of art, architecture or theatre design. But other disciplines such as painting, sculpture, print making or industrial design are also represented. The essential, however, is the ability to draft and use a scale rule, with experience of mechanical drawing.

b) Scenic Artists

Scenic artists are responsible for the painting of backcloths and gauzes and all decorative set features, including floor designs, as specified by the designer. Art work also includes the representation of tapestries, curtains and carpets, the painting of special portraits or pictures in a particular style. Art school training to degree level is essential, together with a knowledge of the styles of different historical periods. Previous experience in television, theatre or films is usually required, though very occasionally someone might be accepted as a trainee.

c) Graphic Design Assistants

These work with graphic designers, who design and supervise the execution of title sequences, credits and all programme graphic material. Training to degree level in graphic design at an art school or equivalent is required, together with some experience in advertising, publishing or allied fields.

d) Graphic Assistants

This job involves work in liaison with graphic designers in the graphic design print room on a wide variety of typographic material for television and film production, including credit captions, small signs, labels, etc. Masseely Hot Press print material is used for some of this work, but the operation of advanced electronic character-generators accounts for the majority of it. Experience in one or more aspects of letter assembly and accurate typing are desirable. Art school education is an advantage.

e) Visual Effects Design Assistants
These are responsible for the construction and operation of all types of visual effects. Ideally, candidates should be capable of good presentational drawing combined with workshop experience of construction in wood, metal, plastic, etc. A working knowledge of sculpture, model-making, painting, optics or pyrotechnics is relevant, and a thorough understanding of the fundamentals of physics, chemistry and electricity is very important. Obviously, previous experience of this type of work in film, theatre or television is an advantage here.

Most departments in television design have occasional holiday vacancies, so it is a good idea to keep a look-out for advertisements.

4 Costume Design Assistants

As well as assisting the costume designer, the assistant may also have to maintain contact between artistes and suppliers, arrange fittings, carry out research work and shop for fabric samples. Applicants should have had training to degree level in theatre or fashion design and have covered the history of costume. Experience in theatre, film, costumiers or other costume work is necessary even for short-term contracts. Also in the costume design team will be a senior dresser and a dresser. Their duties are the maintenance of costumes and dressing of artistes for performances. They must be able to sew and have experience in the theatre, theatrical costumiers or in the film industry. The minimum age is 20.

5 Musicians

BBC Television has a small number of music producers in its Music Programmes Department. Any applicants for vacancies in this field must prove not only that they are musically qualified but also that they have visual imagination and some knowledge of production. Quite a tall order for a newcomer! But if anyone can come up with a really new way to present music visually, maybe they could get a sympathetic ear.

6 News Trainees

Since the scheme began in 1970, more than 150 journalists have found jobs as writers, news editors, producers, presenters, correspondents and reporters. The training course lasts two years, but offers only 12 places a year. It is highly competitive, for there are usually more than 1,000 applicants every year. Most people apply direct from university, but if you have a good academic standard, equivalent to a degree, you may be considered. The main thing is to have a proven commitment to journalism, substantiated by newspaper or magazine cuttings or radio/video tapes of your work. Shorthand and typing are obligatory, of course, before you start training.

7 Production Trainees

Still, I suppose, the top people's way into BBC Television. The scheme offers graduates the opportunity to compete for two years' comprehensive training and experience, mainly in factual programme production. You will have to show evidence of originality of idea and attitude; the ability to generate programme ideas within production teams and argue their merit; to assimilate rapid briefings for research and development; to work quickly and reliably with initiative, often under heavy pressure of time; to write swiftly and accurately. There are 15 places on the course and, at the end of two years, you will be able to apply for researcher or assistant producer jobs. More importantly, however, by having received as part of your training an appreciation of all aspects of the BBC's work and structure, you will lay down for yourself a good foundation if your ambitions lie towards the higher echelons of management.

BBC Television is such a vast and complex organisation with such a prodigious output of programmes that it has been only possible to suggest some of the job prospects. There are many more entry points which might at first seem remote from the sharp end of production but which will nevertheless give a new entrant inside knowledge of the workings of television and the chance to meet others involved in different aspects of production. Some of the areas not covered above are Accounts, Secretarial and Clerical, Computing, News Typists, Librarians and Television Make-up.

One thing you should do is to get hold of some of the excellent literature published by the BBC, so that you can see in detail the opportunities in the departments where you think you may have something to offer. For further information on any BBC jobs apart from Engineering and Technical Operations apply to:

BBC Corporate Recruitment Services
Broadcasting House
London W1A 1AA

ENGINEERING AND TECHNICAL OPERATIONS

The BBC is widely regarded as a world leader in television broadcasting and not least for its advanced engineering and technical standards. Through its network of local, regional and national services, it provides hundreds of hours of programmes each week, and it is the Engineers and Technical Operators who provide the facilities required for the production and transmission of these programmes.

With the expansion of cable and satellite programming, the demand for qualified technicians may well grow considerably. Although this book is aimed primarily at those with ambitions to be involved in the creative processes of film and television, there can be as much job satisfaction in technical wizardry, and there are many cases of people with an engineering or operational background becoming successful directors or producers. To start in Engineering or Technical Operations demands strictly defined educational qualifications and it is worth noting that 30 per cent of the trainee intake are graduates.

1   Technical Operations

a) Trainee Camera Operators

Television camerapersons could be called the eyes of the viewer; they interpret the creative ideas originating from the production people. Trainee camera operators are the junior members of the camera team, working closely with other production staff in studios and occasionally on Outside Broadcasts. The basic skills involve assembly and preparation of equipment before a rehearsal or transmission begins and, during the programme, assisting and driving camera cranes, as well as camera operation. Trainee camera operators need to have a good understanding of both the technical capabilities of the camera and also of the limitations of the medium in which they work. A well-developed sense of the artistic requirements of the production team is essential. In order to undertake the training course you need a good general education, but it is also important that you are oriented towards a real and practical interest in photography, stage lighting and simple electronics.

Trainee camera operators, like all trainees in Technical Operations, start their employment with an initial 10-week introductory course at the BBC's own training centre at Evesham in Worcestershire. After the successful completion of this, training continues 'on the job' until late in the third year, when trainees take another course at Evesham.

b) Trainee Lighting and Vision Control Assistant

The team responsible for the lighting of a television production consists of a lighting director, lighting and vision control supervisor, and a lighting and vision assistant. Much of the assistant's training is on the job, getting to know the equipment and its capabilities, learning to line up the vision control monitoring facilities and operate remote camera controls which adjust the final balance. Trainees also work at the vision control desk and need to develop an eye for a good picture. It is this artistic ability, combined with knowledge of the equipment, which can eventually lead to promotion to lighting and vision control supervisor and even lighting director.

c) Trainee Sound Operators

Sound operators are the people who prepare and operate the sound equipment used in television. In studios, trainee operators track, position and operate sound booms, position microphones and adjust loudspeakers. In control rooms they operate tape recorders and disc reproducers. While the majority of the work occurs inside the studio, occasionally Outside Broadcasts or location work is involved. Trainee sound operators need a good understanding of both the technical capabilities of the sound equipment used and also the limitations of the medium in which they work. A well developed sense of the artistic requirements of the production team is essential.

d) Trainee Recording Operators

Prior to the introduction of videotape recording, the great majority of programmes were broadcast live. Now videotape recorders yield pictures indistinguishable from the original and are the key to the most complex editing and post-production techniques, which in turn can provide a new dimension in programme style. Parallel progress has been made in telecine equipment. Recording operators are the people who operate all this equipment and trainees will therefore be involved with many aspects of programme production, from initial recording to assisting with editing and post-production.

e) Trainee Regional Technical Operators

The BBC produces programmes of news and general features of local interest in Newcastle, Leeds, Norwich, Southampton and Plymouth. Operators in these regional stations need a wide range of skills and trainee operators therefore receive comprehensive training covering most aspects of television operations, from camera operating to setting up sound equipment, from operating electronic processing equipment to testing and aligning studio equipment in conjunction with engineers.

f) Trainee News Technical Operators

As with regional technical operators, news technical operators' work involves sound, recording and camera operations. If you like the idea of working in the live, immediate atmosphere of news programmes, together with a chance to work on a wide range of different activities, this could be the job for you.

g) Trainee Audio Assistants
Each regional station of the BBC has its own audio unit, who work with the camera operators and other members of the studio team. They are involved not only with programme production, both in the studio and on Outside Broadcasts, but also with post-production work spanning television and radio. A trainee gets experience of a wide range of audio equipment and the work may involve rigging studio equipment, recording orchestral concerts, providing sound effects and editing audio tapes.

The qualifications for all jobs in Technical Operations are that you should have a good general education with O-level or equivalent passes in physics, mathematics and English language. Further education is an additional advantage since, as I said before, 30 per cent of trainees nowadays are graduates. In any case you must possess normal hearing and colour vision and since irregular hours are involved you must be at least eighteen. In addition to educational qualifications, the BBC are looking for people with bright, lively minds, artistic flair and a practical approach to problems. It is also very important that you should have a developed interest in relevant hobbies such as photography, stage lighting or audio work, which might involve experience working in hospital radio or operating discos and similar equipment. The training for all Technical Operators lasts for three years and starts with a ten-week introductory course at the BBC's Training Centre at Evesham. Provided you pass this, training continues on the job. After a year your work will be assessed and if satisfactory your appointment will be confirmed. Training continues for the next two years and during the final year another four-week course is taken. On successful completion of the three-year programme you will become a qualified Technical Operator.

2 Engineering

The principal areas where Engineering trainees might be employed are:

a) Television Studio Engineering
Trainee engineers are employed mainly in studios in or near London and their duties include elementary fault diagnosis, repair, modification and construction of equipment. They also carry out operational alignment of cameras, vision mixers, video effects equipment, lighting control systems, electronic graphics equipment, sound control desks and tape recorders.

b) Television Recording
Trainees are involved in the maintenance of recording and reproduction equipment which uses film or magnetic tape.

c) Television News, Current Affairs and Outside Broadcasts
Each has its own Engineering and Technical Resources. Trainees are involved in the line-up and maintenance of equipment and may assist with operations.

d) Television Network
This department, in which trainees are involved in all sections, ensures that sound and vision signals are fed to and received from the various networks (BBC1 and BBC2, UK contribution network, Eurovision and the worldwide satellite system). They also maintain the equipment, which, besides cameras and other studio equipment, includes standards convertors, synchronisers and the CEEFAX computer.

e) Film Engineering
This department services film and electronic cameras, portable audio and videotape recorders, dubbing, transfer and editing equipment. It can also be involved in the design and construction of special facilities to meet programme needs.

Training in all the above posts starts with a familiarisation course at the BBC Training Centre at Evesham. Provided students successfully complete this initial course, they continue to train on the job until they have served for three years, when normally they take a second course at Evesham.

Applicants for trainee Engineering posts must have a good standard of education, including O-level English plus study to A-level in maths and physics. Alternatively, a B/TEC diploma in an electronics-based subject, including level III maths, will be considered. The BBC also recruits each year a large number of graduates in electronic engineering.

Vacancies in Engineering and Technical Operations are normally advertised in the press as they arise, though the BBC do say that they welcome enquiries at any time. If you are still at school or college, you should write *four months* before completing your studies to:

Head of Engineering and Technical Operations Recruitment, BBC, P.O. Box 2 BL, London W1A 2BL, telephone 01 580 4468.

If you apply, remember it is important that you fill in your application form as fully as possible. After all, at the short-listing stage all they know about you is what you tell them.

There are a great number of variations and additions to all the Engineering and Technical Operations opportunities which may occur (for example, in BBC Regions or in Research), and as vacancies may exist at any time applications may be made all the year round. Application forms can also be obtained from universities and polytechnic Career Advisory Services, and additionally the BBC visit many universities and polytechnics during the Lent term to hold campus interviews.

As I have said, a high percentage of Engineering and Technical Operations trainees are graduates, and so in a highly competitive climate there is no doubt that higher education will place you at a distinct advantage; it may also give you opportunities to develop the sort of hobbies which will convince an interviewer that you are really keen to be involved in this side of television. The BBC even runs schemes for those studying or planning to study for degrees in electronics and electrical engineering or physics with an appropriate electronics content. And they have pre-university industrial and vacation training schemes for suitable undergraduates.

The unique advantage of starting your career at the BBC is that they

49

provide training which is wide-ranging, practical and efficient, and the subsequent career path is more strictly defined than in other areas of film and television. There is no comparable centralised training scheme for new entrants to Independent Television Companies. Each company recruits individually and vacancies are pretty scarce. For example, in 1985 only 967 newcomers were taken on by all the ITV companies, of which 271 were in administrative areas, 42 in engineering, 14 in camera departments, and only one a director. But as I've suggested, it is sometimes possible to move from administration to production, and you are certainly better placed when you are on the inside to get to know the jargon and the production people.

As far as training is concerned, the ITV companies concentrate mostly on 'on the job' training, though some are making great efforts to train more trainers. Once you are in, of course, there are increasingly opportunities for further training on courses run by the ITVA or on so-called short courses at the National Film and Television School. The ITVA also arranges for people to attend courses at places like Ravensbourne College of Design and Communications.

8

Training

One route by which you are guaranteed membership of the ACTT (once you have subsequently got a job) and which is still to be recommended whatever the political climate is to graduate from one of the schools and colleges which are recognised by the union. And this brings us to the whole question of training. There has recently been something of an explosion in the entire training sector, and many schools reach an extremely high technical and creative standard with their students. But, unlike some other industries, good qualifications do not in themselves guarantee that employers will be queuing up to employ you. I recently heard of a case of a film from a well-known school annexed to a College of Art which was nominated for the BAFTA Short Film Award. The student who directed it complained that he was without a job for two years after leaving college, which might suggest that he had been selling himself in rather an immodest way, expecting to be employed straight away as a director in an established company. On the other hand a former stills photographer, after graduating from the National Film and Television School, where he had shown enormous talent, was content to take a job as a documentary camera assistant.

In most cases, graduates from a school or college are still faced with the task of trekking round whichever part of the industry is, in their view, likely to prove fruitful, and this may mean taking on very humble jobs. But with good training behind you (plus the necessary talent), you ought to be in a position to advance more rapidly than those who have opted to learn skills while on the job.

Places which offer training fall broadly into the following categories:

1. Courses offering entry at O-level or equivalent.
2. Courses offering entry at A-level or equivalent (mainly colleges of further education and polytechnics).
3. Postgraduate courses.
4. Workshops.
5. Commercially-run courses.

You will find particulars of these in *Directions* and in *Film & Television Training*, both published by the British Film Institute, in *Careers in Independent Television* published by the ITVA, and in *Education and Training for Film and Television*, published by BKSTS. (See the bibliography for further details.)

Training courses of various kinds, chiefly vocational, are also offered by trade organisations and commercial companies, such as the Royal Television Society, the British Kinematograph, Sound and Television Society (BKSTS) and Kodak. For further details see the list of addresses at the end of this book.

There is no doubt that the National Film and Television School at Beaconsfield in Bucks has the most consistently high reputation of all the schools, so let's look at the qualifications for entry, and the aims and philosophy of the courses. The objects for which the school is established are broad; among the recommendations of the committee originally set up to institute the school are that:

The school should provide for all the creative aspects of film-making such as producing, directing, editing, camera-work, screen-writing and design.

Training should not concentrate on only one type of film-making such as feature films, but should regard all types of films as within its province.

The content of the course should be strongly professional, while at the same time being broadly based on a background of humane studies relevant to the art of the cinema. On the practical side, each student should have the opportunity during the course of making a number of films of various kinds.

What, then, are the qualifications for admission? To quote from the School's own prospectus: 'It is to be expected that some successful candidates will have a high level of academic training, but this will not be decisive. The School functions at the level of a postgraduate course, although a first degree is not a requirement of admission. It is left largely to the initiative of applicants to make their candidacy as persuasive as possible, bearing in mind the general objectives of the school, and the specific area of work for which the applicant is a candidate.'

The School has departments for animation, art direction, camera, documentary, editing, film music composition, production, script and sound. So applicants have first to choose one of these areas, and must submit evidence to convince the interviewing panel that they are worthy of one of the small number of places available in each category. It is expected that applications will be supported by examples of work such as films, videos, still photographs, short stories or plays, work in the theatre, in a film club or at another film school or university.

The three-year course selects about 30 students each year, more or less equally divided between men and women. This is certainly not a course for beginners, but being professionally based, with a staff largely consisting of eminent practitioners, the National Film and Television School provides an outstanding foundation for a career in film or television. And with the establishment of the National Short Course Training Programme (NSCTP), which operates as a separate unit on the School's premises, there is now the chance to take follow-up courses while you are working in the industry.

There is a new kind of apprenticeship scheme for certain grades in film-making, called JOBFIT, which stands for Joint Board for Film Industry Training. It was jointly set up by the ACTT, the British Film and Television Producers Association (BFTPA) and the Independent Programme Producers Association (IPPA). The Advertising Film and Video Producers Association (AFVPA) and Channel Four are also sponsors. JOBFIT is part of the UK Network for Independent Film, Television and Video Training, which also includes CYFLE, the equivalent body for Wales, NEMDC (North East Media Development Council), the Scottish Film Training Trust and NSCTP. (See the BFI publication *Directions*, listed in the bibliography, for further details.)

One of the complaints from people working in the industry when employing graduates from film schools is that students think only about becoming producers, directors or perhaps camerapersons, and lose patience quickly when faced with the more menial jobs such as clapper/loader, or third assistant director (often a glorified tea-maker). Equally, those who have managed to land a job without going through film school find it impossible to get any formal training.

To quote their own publicity, JOBFIT aims:

To create the first systematic, industry-wide training scheme covering ACTT film technician grades, for new entrants into the free-lance sector. The scheme is an equal opportunity initiative.

In essence the style is that of an apprenticeship where trainees will be attached to film productions over a two-year period. Supporting college-based training will also be provided.

JOBFIT will train up to 50 people per year. Trainees will be taken on in groups of twelve, at intervals, and be contracted to JOBFIT for two years, subject to regular reviews and assessment. On satisfactory completion of the training programme trainees will receive ACTT membership, in a junior grade of their chosen specialist area.

Training will be specifically in technical and production grades of film-making covered by the ACTT, i.e. Art Department Assistant, Assistant Script Supervisor, Assistant Boom Operator, Clapper/Loader, Assistant Sound Recordist, Third Assistant Director, Second Assistant Editor, etc.

Trainees will be attached to a variety of film productions, ranging across features, documentaries, specialised film-making and commercials. Throughout the two years, on-the-job experience will be supplemented by formal technical training in the form of blocks of 3-4 week courses at recognised film and television training centres.

The first year is designed as a general training period during which trainees will be attached to a number of different departments in the film-making process, i.e. Art Department, Production, Editorial, Camera, Sound, etc. During this period trainees will gain experience of the work done by different film technicians involved in the production process. In their second year trainees will specialise in one area. The choice of this specialist area will be determined by personal aptitudes and job opportunities in the industry.

JOBFIT hopes to extend eventually to cover all junior production grades, and there is also a need for a similar initiative in other craft areas of film and television such as plasterers, props, grips, make-up and wardrobe. JOBFIT was set up for trainees in the feature film industry and in filmed commercials. There is also a modest initiative, financed by Channel Four and administered by JOBFIT, to take on a few trainees who are members of ethnic minorities and attach them to independent companies who operate entirely on videotape. These lucky few will concentrate largely on camera, sound and editing techniques, although the scheme may be extended to researchers. The two-year training period will consist of one year working with a company and one year's more formal training through short courses at the National Film and Television School. If the experiment is successful it may be extended beyond the initial five trainees. For more particulars contact Gill Monk, Channel Four, 60 Charlotte Street, London W1P 2AX.

Of the courses which are entirely electronically- as opposed to film-based, those at Ravensbourne College of Design and Communication at Bromley in Kent are very well established. The two full-time two-year courses are B/TEC HND in Engineering (Communications) for Television and Broadcasting, and B/TEC HND in Design Communication (Television Programme Operations). The first is an electronic engineering-based course designed to give the student sufficient information and training to follow a career in such areas as electronic maintenance, broadcast studio design, quality control, etc. The second is aimed specifically at people wanting to operate technical equipment in the radio, television and recording industries. The kinds of jobs the course might lead to are vision mixer, sound balance engineer, camera operator or videotape editor.

Many of Ravensbourne's students are already employed by ITV companies in some capacity and are doing conversion or familiarisation courses, or they may be attending one of Ravensbourne's short courses in Basic Television Studio Operations, VTR Operational Technology or Colour Television Engineering.

This close relationship with the ITV companies means that other Ravensbourne students often have the chance to do holiday relief work, thus giving them the chance to experience the sharp end of working in television. But it must be emphasised that the courses are all video- and electronically-based and are therefore less likely to lead to the more creative jobs such as writing, directing or producing. Even so, there is always scope for the really ambitious and talented person armed with the high technical qualifications Ravensbourne provides.

The other side of the coin is represented by the entirely film-based course run by the Film Department of the Royal College of Art in London. The Royal College of Art will not consider you for entry unless you are already a graduate, and in fact it is the only place which runs a postgraduate two-year Master's Degree course in aspects of film production.

A small number (7 in 1987) of students are production scholars and the course aims to create potential producer-director partnerships who, it is hoped, will help form the nucleus of a reinvigorated young feature film industry in Britain. In parallel, there is a general film-making course for about 15 students concentrating on commercials and pop promos, based on the philosophy that in these areas lies the greatest demand for original creative talent in the job market.

There are also courses for a small number in design, divided into 3-D design, which encompasses costumes, sets, and the finding and adaptation of locations; and 2-D design, which covers computer graphics, film and television titles, special effects, and extending into publicity posters.

For graduates who have a leaning towards any of these areas, a Master's Degree from the RCA would be a prestigious qualification, and indeed the places are eagerly sought after. If, however, you are nowhere near becoming a graduate or maybe never likely to be one, but if on the other hand you are one of those lucky people who from an early age know what they want to do, then you should consider the Children's Film Unit. This is for anyone aged between 7 and 16 who already has an over-riding ambition to learn about film production with a view to subsequently making a career in the industry.

The unit was formed as a charity in 1981. Its aims are primarily educational in the broadest sense. It teaches its members the value of teamwork, discipline and self-confidence at the same time as learning and putting into practice all the craft and creative skills of film-making. Although of the hundreds who have attended the Children's Film Unit some have moved on to further training or directly into the industry, and this includes several actors and actresses, this is not the primary aim of the unit.

The actual direction of the films produced is still undertaken by the unit's Artistic Director, Colin Finbow, but the scripting, camerawork, sound, lighting, make-up, set design and editing, as well as many of the front of camera performances, are carried out by the children themselves. Much of the training is done in workshop sessions and here adults are involved in an advisory capacity. Video is used for this part of the work, but the main productions are on 16mm. film.

The unit's films have received enthusiastic screenings at the Institute of Contemporary Arts and have also been shown on Channel Four, who have given valuable support and funding. There is no doubt that access to this type of training and to equipment must be an advantage to someone seeking subsequent entry into regular training establishments, or even to someone trying to get a foot in the door of a production organisation. But beware of the pitfall of suggesting to any potential employer that you know it all. Sell yourself by all means and don't hold back on the enthusiasm – your experience and talent should become apparent all in good time after you've landed the job or film school place!

Contact the Children's Film Unit at Studio 4, 192 Queenstown Road, Battersea, London SW8 3NR.

There are many other colleges and establishments providing training in film and television; they are listed in the publications referred to in the bibliography. But besides the National Film and Television School, the only other ones at present recognised by the ACTT are the London International Film School, West Surrey College of Art and Design, the London College of Printing, the Polytechnic of Central London, Bournemouth and Poole College of Art and Design and the Drama Department of the University of Bristol.

You will have to make up your own mind, whether to devote time to following a course (always provided you have the necessary qualifications) in the hope that the benefits will pay off in the long run, or

57

whether it is preferable to get your apprenticeship 'on the job'. Taking the latter course will certainly teach you the down-to-earth practicality and hard slog of the commercial world of film and television, while at the same time allowing you to study at closer quarters the work of top creative professionals. On the other hand, film schools give you the opportunity to carry out the whole creative process at an earlier stage and in a more unfettered way than may ever be possible as a professional.

Talking of my intention to write this book to a friend who is a documentary director with a long and distinguished record, he observed drily that it should be a very short volume consisting of just one page: 'Advice to those wanting to get into the Film and Television Industries – don't!'

Nevertheless, to the vast majority of us, in spite of recurrent crises, periods of bad luck and frustration at not being able to achieve what we should like, deep down we would not want to follow any other career: in fact for most of us it is more than merely a career, it is an obsession and some might even go so far as to say a 'calling', which, when a production goes right, can be enormously stimulating and satisfying to all the team concerned in its creation. One thing it never is – dull.

So to those who are keen to be part of the business in one form or another, I can only say that there *is* room for those with persistence, ideas and talent and newcomers with these attributes are essential to the success of Films and Television, whatever direction they take in the future.

Postscript: How They Got Started

A random selection of well-known people in film and television describe how they first got into the business:

Jeremy Isaacs, the first Chief Executive of Channel Four: 'My first job was as a researcher, writing the weather forecast for Granada Television. I got it by using introductions to friends of a friend of a friend, and by demonstrating what I could do by some written and broadcast journalism of a basic but practical sort.'

Sydney Samuelson CBE, Chairman and Chief Executive, Samuelson Group of Companies: 'My start in the industry came when I managed to get a job as rewind boy at a cinema which had just been built in my local town of Lancing in Sussex. I wrote to the manager with the approach of my fourteenth birthday and was originally offered the job of page boy, but I did not fancy wearing the obligatory pill-box hat and could see no reason why I should not start on the bottom-but-one rung of the ladder.'

David Puttnam, formerly Chairman and Chief Executive, Columbia Pictures: 'When I left school at sixteen, I wanted to go into films but took a job as a messenger with a publisher and then moved on to be a messenger for an advertising agency. By the time I was twenty-two I'd been through three agencies and was in charge of the Acrilan account. But when I refused to work on the Benson and Hedges account, I borrowed £3,000 of the agency's money to help set up a photographer's agency. It was so successful that it enabled me to set up

Goodtimes Enterprises with Sandy Lieberson and keep going for a year or so until Rothschilds came in and took up the slack.'

Verity Lambert, producer of *Rock Follies, Edward and Mrs Simpson, The Naked Civil Servant, Comfort and Joy,* etc: 'My first job was as a secretary for Granada Television. ITV was just starting up so there were quite a few jobs available and I was looking for something that was interesting and not too bothered about it being 9 to 5.30.'

Arthur Wooster, lighting cameraman of *Eat the Peach,* director-cameraman on second unit of *The Living Daylights, A View to a Kill, Octopussy:* 'A friend of my father was studio manager of the Army Kinematograph Services at Wembley Studios and he got me an introduction to Chick Fowle at the Crown Film Unit, where I got taken on as a clapper boy.'

Richard Marden, editor of *Sunday, Bloody Sunday* (BAFTA Award), *Two for the Road, Bedazzled, Sleuth:* 'My father worked for GEC, who supplied electrical stuff to Walton Studios. He knew Bill Norris there very well and he recommended me for a job as a trainee in the sound department of Kays' Carlton Hill Studios. My first job was sweeping out the sound truck.'

John Glen, director of *The Living Daylights, A View to a Kill, Octopussy* and other James Bond films: 'I started as an office boy at Shepperton Studios. I just called at the main gate and got to see the personnel people. Just when I'd given up hope of hearing any more, they called me. A bit later I became a runner in the cutting rooms and then a numbering boy. From then on I gradually worked my way into a cutting room.'

Roger Deakins, lighting cameraman on *Another Time, Another Place, 1984, Defence of the Realm, Sid and Nancy, White Mischief:* 'After getting a degree at art college, I spent a year as a photo-journalist. These two things combined to get me a place at the National Film and Television School. When I graduated I tried to get work as a cameraman or camera assistant; the first job I landed was as a documentary cameraman in Rhodesia, as it was then – a film about the war sponsored by the ANC. It was pretty undercover stuff and we had to pretend we were making a travelogue!'

Jim O'Brien, director of *Jewel in the Crown* (seven episodes), *The Monocled Mutineer:* 'I'd been a fringe theatre director before I went to the National Film and Television School. When I graduated I spent months trailing around with my show-reel, and Alan Seymour, a writer/producer who I'd worked with in the theatre and who was now a producer at the BBC, saw it. He took a chance with a new writer, Susan Boyd, and me, a new director, and the result was a drama called *Another Day.* But before this all came together, I got a job for a few weeks as location manager for a commercials company, as I needed the money, being thirty by this time and with two kids!'

John Schlesinger, director of *Billy Liar, Far from the Madding Crowd, Midnight Cowboy, Marathon Man,* etc: 'When I was at Oxford, I directed two amateur films and on leaving became an actor. While I was playing in Peter Hall's *Mourning Becomes Electra* I made a documentary film called *Sunday in the Park,* which was shown on BBC Television. This gave me my first chance in the film industry as a researcher and assistant director on a documentary for World Wide Pictures. I was then offered some documentary films to direct for BBC's *Tonight* and *Monitor* programmes.'

Useful Addresses and Publications

1 Addresses

a) Television Companies:

British Broadcasting Corporation
Portland Place
London W1A 1AA

Anglia Television
Anglia House
Norwich
Norfolk NR1 3JG

Border Television
Television Centre
Carlisle CA1 3NT

Central Independent Television
Central House
Broad Street
Birmingham B1 2JP

Grampian Television
Queen's Cross
Aberdeen AB9 2XJ

Granada Television
Manchester M60 9EA

HTV Wales
Television Centre
Culverhouse Cross
Cardiff CF5 6XJ

HTV West
Television Centre
Bristol BS4 3HG

Independent Television News
ITN House
48 Wells Street
London W1P 4DE

London Weekend Television
South Bank Television Centre
Kent House
Upper Ground
London SE1 9LT

Scottish Television
Cowcaddens
Glasgow G2 3PR

Television South
Television Centre
Vinters Park
Maidstone
Kent ME14 5NZ

Television South West
Derry's Cross
Plymouth
Devon PL1 2SP

Thames Television
306-316 Euston Road
London NW1 3BB

TV-am
Hawley Crescent
London NW1 8EF

Tyne Tees Television
The Television Centre
City Road
Newcastle-upon-Tyne NE1 2AL

Ulster Television
Havelock House
Ormeau Road
Belfast BT7 1EB

Yorkshire Television
The Television Centre
Leeds LS3 1JS

b) Training – contact the following organisations for further information:

BFTPA
Paramount House
162-170 Wardour Street
London W1V 4LA

British Kinematograph, Sound
   and Television Society
(attn. Anne Fenton)
549 Victoria House
Vernon Place
London WC1B 4DJ

IVCA
102 Great Russell Street
London WC1E 3LN

JOBFIT
4th Floor, 5 Dean Street
London W1V 5RN

Kodak Limited
Kodak House
P.O. Box 66
Hemel Hempstead
Hertfordshire HP1 1JU

National Association for Higher
   Education in Film and Video
Faculty of Art and Design
Harrow College of Higher
   Education
Northwick Park
Watford Road
Harrow HA1 3TP

National Film and
   Television School
Beaconsfield Studios
Station Road
Beaconsfield
Bucks HP9 1LG

Royal Television Society
Tavistock House East
Tavistock Square
London WC1H 9HR

2 Publications

a) The following are available from BFI Publications, 21 Stephen Street, London W1P 1PL:

Directions
A regularly updated listing of short training courses in film and video. Price £2.00 (£2.40 inc p & p).

Film & Television Training
A guide to undergraduate and postgraduate training in film and television production. Price £2.75 (£3.00 inc p & p).

Studying Film & Television
A guide to academic courses on television and the cinema. Price £2.75 (£3.00 inc p & p). This publication and the one above are available together price £4.50 (£5.00 inc p & p).

Film and Television Handbook 1989-90
Contains addresses and details of currently active film production companies, facilities houses, workshops, etc. Price £10.95 approx. (£11.95 inc p & p).

b) Other publications include:

Careers in ITV, available from the ITVA Training Department, Knighton House, 56 Mortimer Street, London W1N 8AN, price £4 (inc p & p).

Education and Training for Film and Television, available from British Kinematograph Sound and Television Society, 547-549 Victoria House, Vernon Place, London WC1B 4DJ, price £2.50 (inc p & p).

Kay's UK Production Manual 1987 (London: B L Kay Publishing Co.); biennial UK directory of film, video and television companies.

Kemp's International Film and Television Yearbook 1987-88 (London: Kemp's Printing and Publishing Co.); information on companies and technical services in the UK and abroad.

Screen International Film and TV Yearbook (London: King Publications); directory of British film and television, including cinemas, studios and production companies.

Broadcast Yearbook and Diary 1987 (London: International Thomson); contains information on British television industry.